MAKING
KITES

MAKING
KITES

How to build and fly your very own kites - from simple sleds to complex stunters

RHODA BAKER & MILES DENYER

CHARTWELL
BOOKS, INC.

A QUINTET BOOK

Published by Chartwell Books
A Division of Book Sales, Inc.
110 Enterprise Avenue
Secaucus, New Jersey 07094

This edition produced for sale
in the U.S.A., its territories
and dependencies only.

ISBN 1-55521-840-7

This book was designed and produced by
Quintet Publishing Limited
6 Blundell Street
London N7 9BH

Creative Director: Richard Dewing
Designer: Pete Laws
Project Editors: Bill Hemsley/Katie Preston
Editor: Jenny Millington
Photographer: Jeremy Thomas

Typeset in Great Britain by
Central Southern Typesetters, Eastbourne
Manufactured in Singapore by
Eray Scan Pte Limited
Printed in Hong Kong by
Leefung-Asco Printers Limited

Acknowledgements
The Publishers would also like to thank Gill Bloom for
supplying the pictures on pages 7, 9 and 21 and the
Ann Ronan Picture Library at Image Select for
supplying the pictures on page 11.

CONTENTS

INTRODUCTION

THE EARLY HISTORY OF KITES

Kites originated in Asia and were probably invented in China about 3,000 years ago. Kite flying may also have developed independently among the islands of Micronesia in the South Pacific. From China, the secret of kite building quickly spread to Korea, Japan, Malaysia and India, countries where kites are still very popular today.

It is unclear when kites first appeared in Europe, but they may have been known to the ancient Greeks. They were certainly in use by the time of the Battle of Hastings in 1066, when strings of kites were flown as battle signals. The English name – kite – is taken from the kite, a graceful bird of prey.

RITUAL

In Asia, kites have often had a ritual or religious significance. Many Chinese kites were built to represent the dragons of Chinese folklore. Other traditional designs include birds, butterflies and even centipedes.

In Malaysia, kites flying over a house at night are believed to keep away evil spirits. In Korea, the name of a newborn child is often inscribed on a kite, which is then released to the wind. The Koreans believe that the kite carries with it any evil spirits that attended the child's birth. To find such a kite is thought to bring bad luck.

Kite-flying in Japan has always been a social activity. The inhabitants of a village would often cooperate to build one huge kite. These village kites measured up to 120 square yards in surface area, and could be flown only at festivals because they needed all the villagers to launch them.

SPORT

Kites were also used for sport, and kite-fighting is still very popular, especially in India and Thailand. Indian fighting kites have powdered glass glued to the line. The idea is to use the glass to cut through the line of an opponent's kite.

In Thailand, kite-fighting is a team sport. Contests take place between one large, star-shaped *chula* kite, and several smaller, diamond-shaped *pakpao* kites. The aim is to entangle an opposing kite and drag it to the ground. In addition to providing entertainment, these contests are supposed to make the rainy monsoon winds blow away.

Kite-fighting has also become popular in several South American countries. Razor-blades are attached to the framework of the kite, and contestants try to batter and slash each others' kites in mid-air.

WARFARE

The peoples of Asia soon realized that kites produce considerable "lift," and could be used for carrying ropes across rivers when building a bridge. Large kites could even lift humans, which meant that they could be used in warfare.

As early as 169 B.C., a Chinese general is said to have sent soldiers aloft on kites to observe a besieged city and estimate the length of tunnel needed to reach the city walls. Old Japanese prints show archers suspended from kites shooting down at the enemy beneath.

Kites had even more sinister uses. The 13th-century explorer Marco Polo relates how Chinese sea captains would send a prisoner aloft on a kite when trying to decide whether to set sail. If the prisoner was safely returned to earth, then the omens for the voyage were good. If, however, the prisoner failed to survive, the voyage was postponed. Fortunately, this method of weather forecasting has since been superseded.

AERIAL ARTISTS?

The Nazca people of ancient Peru carved a great network of lines and pictures into the flat desert landscape. Most of the pictures are so big that they cannot be appreciated from the ground. The designs make sense only when viewed from the air. The pictures have puzzled scientists ever since they were discovered. Some people have claimed that the work was carried out by visitors from outer space. Another theory suggests that the pictures were designed by artist-priests suspended from kites, although there is no other evidence of kite flying in South America at this time. It is otherwise accepted that kites did not reach America until after its "discovery" by Europeans in 1492.

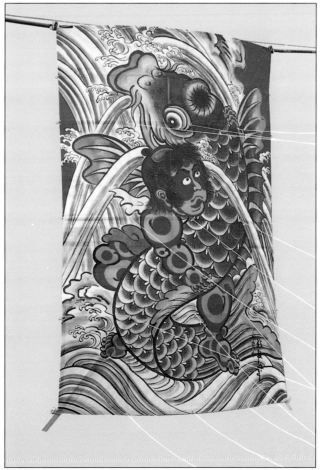

Above

Kites, like those shown, flying in train can reach spectacular heights.

Left

A modern kite which uses a traditional Asian motif and design.

LATER DEVELOPMENTS

In Europe kites became children's playthings, but they did not attract serious attention until the 18th century. In 1749 the Scottish scientist Alexander Wilson used a series of kites with thermometers attached to measure the air temperature at different altitudes.

Three years later, in 1752, Benjamin Franklin carried out his famous experiment to prove that lightning was electricity. By flying a kite during a thunderstorm, he showed that electricity passed down the string when he received a shock from a key attached to the lower end. In fact, Franklin was extremely lucky to survive because this was a very dangerous experiment. The electricity from the lightning could quite easily have killed him.

Kites continued to be used for exploring the atmosphere until the early 20th century, when they were superseded by balloons, airplanes and, eventually, satellites.

IDEA OF FLIGHT

In 1804, after flying a kite with a curved surface, the Englishman Sir George Cayley developed the idea of untethered heavier-than-air flight. Later he built a large, kite-shaped glider that succeeded in carrying his servant across a valley.

At the end of the 19th century, Wilbur and Orville Wright used kites to test their ideas for a flying machine. In 1903 they made the first-ever powered flight.

Meanwhile, tethered kite flights had become all the rage in Europe and America, and were a popular attraction at fairs and shows. The Anglo-American Samuel Cody, the flamboyant Wild West showman, used kites to tow himself across the English Channel.

The inventor of the telephone, Alexander Graham Bell, also designed a tetrahedronal kite made of pyramid-shaped cells. In 1907 one of his kites (containing 3,393 individual cells) lifted a man to a height of 170 feet when towed behind a small steamship.

PRACTICAL PURPOSES

Beyond the idea of flight itself, kites also had a number of other practical (and not so practical) uses.

In 1827 the Englishman George Pocock used a pair of large kites to tow a wheeled carriage, or "flying chariot," at speeds of up to 20 mph. For quite obvious reasons, the idea never caught on. In 1847 a child's kite was used during the construction of a suspension bridge across the Niagara River.

The Italian Guglielmo Marconi used a kite to lift an aerial high enough for him to receive the first transatlantic radio signal in 1901. Five years later, kites were used to take aerial photographs of the damage caused by the 1906 San Francisco earthquake.

In 1919 a train of eight kites flown from Germany reached an altitude of nearly 6½ miles. An early science-fiction writer even suggested that kites could be used to carry people to the moon!

WORLD WAR II

During World War II, kites were used for a variety of different purposes: as observation platforms towed behind ships and submarines; as targets for training antiaircraft gunners; and as part of the survival pack for aircrew who went down at sea. The *Gibson Girl* kite hoisted a radio aerial so that a distress message could be transmitted.

AEROBATIC KITES

Since World War II, there has been a resurgence of interest in kite-flying just for the fun of it. This interest has been stimulated by the introduction of new kite designs that can perform controlled aerobatic maneuvers.

In 1948 Francis Rogallo patented his Flexi-wing kite, which was also the forerunner of the modern hang-glider and microlight aircraft.

Domina Jalbert designed the aerodynamic parafoil in 1964; this can be used both as a kite and as a parachute. Parafoiling behind speedboats has become a popular attraction at beach resorts.

In 1975 Peter Powell introduced his dual-line stunt kite, which opened up a whole new world of high-excitement stunt-kiting.

Left

An American, Woodbridge Davis, devised a kite in 1894 for reaching shipwrecks. The kite carried a rescue line which was used to bring a breeches-buoy to the survivors.

Below

In Switzerland in 1844, Dr. Colladon was also investigating the lifting power of the kite. A dummy, sitting in a wicker chair, was blown along a kite line by means of a large umbrella.

FLYING A SINGLE-LINE KITE

Select a suitable open flying area clear of obstructions and buildings that can create air turbulence. Smooth launching requires a steady air-flow. If flying on a hillside, choose the windward side of the hill.

Check that your kite is correctly assembled – that the struts are secure; that the bridle is properly positioned for flying; that the tail (if fitted) is unfurled; and that the line is not tangled.

LAUNCHING

The worst way to launch a kite is to run with it. If the wind has moderate speed, it is easy to self-launch a kite.

Stand with your back to the wind, with the handle in one hand and the kite in the other. Hold the kite up at arm's length and release it, unwinding some line as you do so. Let out more line as the kite rises.

In light winds, you may need a helper to assist you with a long-launch. With your back to the wind, ask the helper to take the kite and walk backwards for 30–50 feet. Unwind line as he or she does so. At your signal, the helper should release the kite, while you pull in some line to help the kite to rise.

FLYING TIPS

If the kite has difficulty gaining height, you can winch it up. Allow some line out, so that the kite falls. Just before it touches the ground, quickly reel in the line, causing the kite to climb. Repeat until the kite has sufficient altitude.

If the kite suddenly starts to dive, don't panic and don't pull. Let out more line, and the kite will probably right itself. To avoid crashing your kite, release the handle and line about a yard before it hits the ground to give a softer landing.

If the lines of two kites cross, don't pull. Both fliers should walk toward each other until the lines uncross.

The standard way to land a kite is to pull in all the line with both hands, making sure a tangle does not form at your feet. With large and hard-pulling kites, you may need to walk the kite down, running a gloved hand along the line.

Right
To self-launch a kite, hold the kite vertically by the bottom edge and release it, letting out a little line.

If self-launching isn't successful, try a long launch. Give the signal to release the kite and either move backwards or pull the line in.

Wind ▶

Above
If there isn't enough wind to support the kite, use a winch launch to lift the kite gradually.

Hard-pulling kite
▶

Left
Make sure you wear gloves when walking down a hard-pulling kite.

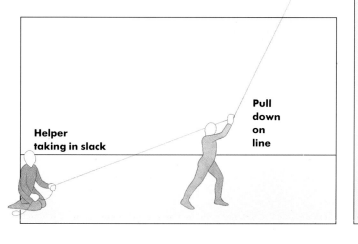

Helper taking in slack

Pull down on line

SAFETY FIRST

Flying kites is a fun, safe pastime as long as you follow a few simple rules:

- Wear gloves when flying kites. In strong winds, larger kites can pull hard enough to cut and burn your hands.
- *Never* fly a kite near overhead cables or in stormy weather. Remember – *electricity can kill.*
- Do not fly kites near airports, airfields, railroad tracks, or major roads. In many countries there are laws to prevent this.
- Never climb trees to retrieve a stranded kite; the branches may not take your weight.
- Always be courteous and helpful to other fliers; do not crowd their flying space.

FLYING A DUAL-LINE STUNT KITE

Unlike a single-line kite, a stunt kite will not stay airborne by itself. Stunt kites need constant attention and control to keep them aloft. Basic control is very simple – you hold one line-handle in each hand; pull on the left-hand line to move the kite to the left, and pull on the right to move right.

Stunt kites can swoop at speeds over 60mph and can therefore be dangerous. Take the greatest care not to hit other fliers or bystanders. If you doubt whether there is enough room to fly your stunt kite, find a larger and more open space.

LAUNCHING

With practice, you can self-launch a stunt kite, but beginners will find it easier with the assistance of a helper. Remember always to keep the wind behind you.

Ask the helper to walk the kite backwards while you unwind the lines. Make sure that they are the same length and do not become crossed or tangled. At your signal, the helper should lift the kite and release it, while you step backwards and pull the kite up into the air. Keep your hands together as the kite rises.

At first, let the kite rise as high as it can and practice basic control. To fly straight, keep both hands together.

FLYING TIPS

The shorter your lines, the faster your reactions have to be in order to keep control. For beginners, lines about 200 feet long will give enough reaction time for practicing.

While practicing, keep your kite away from the ground; otherwise, it may crash and be damaged.

Stunt kites tend to speed up when they near the ground – step forward and slacken the lines in order to reduce speed.

AERIAL MANEUVERS

The simplest maneuver is the loop, performed by gently moving one hand back, pulling on one line. Start with large loops, keeping your hands close together. Smaller loops are made with the hands farther apart. After performing loops in one direction, uncross the lines with an equal number of loops in the other direction.

Other simple maneuvers include the vertical figure-of-eight and the power dive.

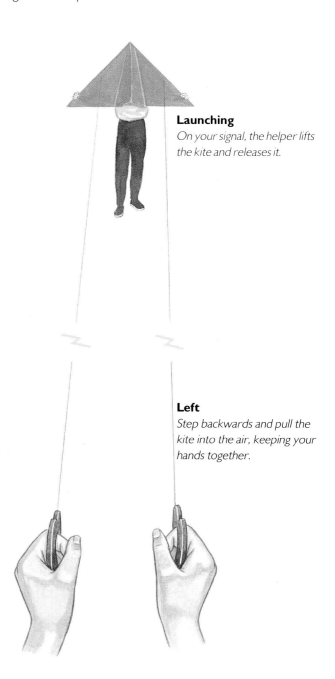

Launching
On your signal, the helper lifts the kite and releases it.

Left
Step backwards and pull the kite into the air, keeping your hands together.

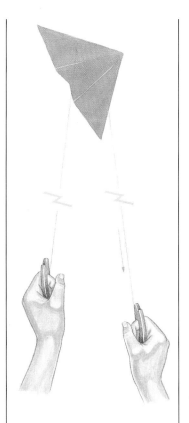

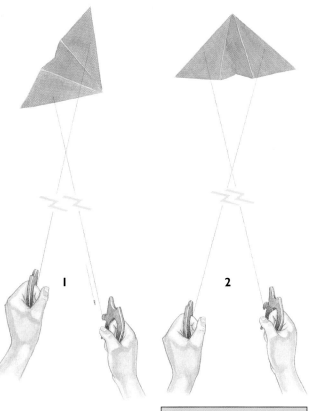

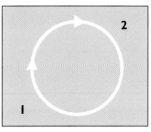

Right turn

Gently pull on the right-hand line to steer to the right.

Left turn

Gently pull on the left-hand line to steer to the left.

Simple loop

1 *Pull back gently on the right-hand line to make the kite loop.*
2 *At the peak of the loop bring your hands level.*

Figure-of-eight

1 *Pull the right-hand line back and then forwards again so that your hands are level.*
2 *Pull the left-hand line back and then bring your hands level.*
3 *Pull your right-hand line back gently to return to the beginning.*

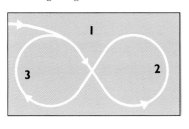

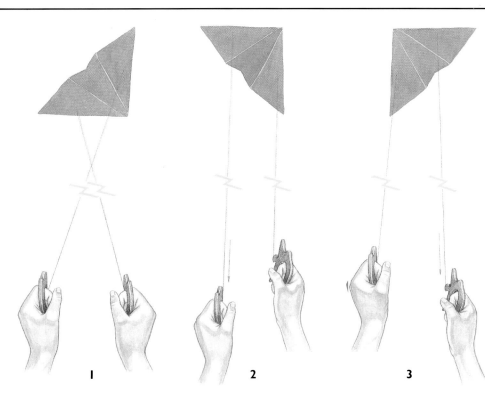

MATERIALS AND EQUIPMENT

We have suggested suitable materials for each of the kites in this book, but these can usually be varied depending on your resources – financial or otherwise! Specialist kite stores will stock wonderful, but more expensive, items – with imagination, these can often be replaced with cheaper substitutes, and the kites will fly just as well. Kites made from alternative materials are best tested in calmer wind conditions – experiment and have fun!

FABRIC, PLASTICS, AND PAPER

Ripstop nylon is the ideal kite-making fabric, being very strong and colorful, but it is expensive and can be hard to find unless you have a local kite store. Kites can be made just as effectively from any strong fabric that doesn't stretch too much, such as cotton, polyester, or even silk.

Simple kites can be made from sheet plastic, which could be a heavy-duty garbage bag cut to shape, or even a plastic shopping bag – a good way to recycle them! Many kites can also be made of ordinary wrapping paper, tissue paper, or even newspaper, and will survive for a surprisingly long time unless they get wet.

SPARS AND FRAMES

Dowel makes a good light frame and is inexpensive – choose ramin hardwood dowel for strength. Kite stores sell the more hi-tech materials such as fiberglass or carbon fiber rods, which will be needed for the stunt kites in this book. Small, lightweight kites may need only a split bamboo-cane or even a drinking-straw frame to fly successfully.

LINES AND KNOTS

There are many different kinds and weights of kite lines available – the best are the braided lines, with twisted lines a cheaper alternative. Most are made from nylon or polyester. The smaller kites can be flown from ordinary thread or light string.

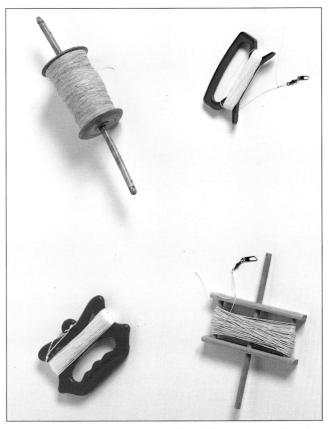

Four different types of handles and reels.

A handle for a lightweight kite need only be plywood with a notch at each end. A simple shape like this can be cut from plywood with a jigsaw, and makes a very good handle and line reel all in one.

HANDLES AND REELS

Again, handles can vary from the expensive, ready-made variety to a simple piece of plywood with a notch at each end to wind the line around. Wooden handles are reasonably easy to make and can be adapted to suit your hand – obviously, strength and comfort are most important. Reels and spools for the flying line are not really essential for any of the simpler kites.

16

Basic equipment
(clockwise from top)
junior hacksaw
marker pens
metal ruler
cellophane tape
sandpaper
pencils
scissors
masking tape
craft knife
needle and thread
pins
glue stick
cutting mat

B R I D L E S

Some kites will fly with just a simple flying line attached – the Box Kite project in this book is an example. Others need a bridle to provide an attachment point for the flying line and to keep the kite in the correct position in the wind. Adjusting the bridle slightly will tilt the kite against the wind and alter the way it flies.

Lowering the towing point when the wind is light will allow more of the kite's surface to catch the wind. In stronger wind conditions, the kite will need to tilt more toward the horizontal, and will need a higher towing point.

Hang the kite from your finger by the bridle point to check its balance. If one side is noticeably heavier, trim the

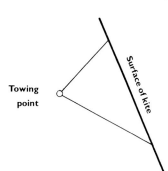

A lower towing point is needed in light wind conditions.

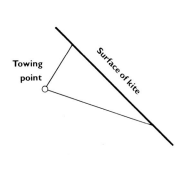

In stronger wind conditions, move the towing point up towards the top of the kite.

decorations until both sides are even. Attach the flying line.

B I T S   A N D   P I E C E S

We have used split rings (like small keyrings) to make the kites described in this book – they are easier to attach to lines and loops than closed, alloy rings, which also cost more. End caps for spars are also available, but not essential – we protect the pockets by wrapping the ends of the spars with tape. A trip around any large hardware store will lead you to plastic tubing, doweling, and many small items such as split rings.

K E E L S

The use of a keel in a bridling system gives very good stability. The keel is a triangle made of the same material as the kite, with the longest side along the spine of the kite. A keel bridle blocks the path of the wind, and so the kite is laterally stable. Two or three alternative towing points can be made at the bottom tip of the keel, for example in the Diamond Keeled kite, which allow for adjustment in different wind conditions.

In addition to providing stability, a keel helps to distribute stress along the whole length of the sail, rather than having stress at the points where the bridle is attached. This means that flight is much smoother and more controlled.

HINTS FOR CONSTRUCTION

All the kites in this book are reasonably straightforward to make: if you are a beginner, start with the easy projects such as the Paperfold Kite or Sled. Follow the steps slowly, and refer to the picture of the finished kite to see what shape you are aiming for.

SAFETY FIRST

When cutting out plastic or tubes with craft knives, remember to use a cutting mat or a thick layer of cardboard to protect the surface you are cutting on. *Never* use a craft knife to cut toward yourself or your free hand – if the blade slips you could suffer serious injury. Keep all sharp equipment safely to one side out of the reach of children, and away from areas where you are likely accidentally to lean on blades or points.

SEWING AND GLUING

Many of the kites in this book can be assembled using just a glue stick – obviously kites that are going to be flown in high winds and used for stunts need stronger construction techniques. Sewn kites can use simple flat seams or the stronger flat-fell seam.

REPAIRS

If you make a mistake during construction, don't despair – usually a repair or patch will be easy to make and won't show at all once the kite is airborne. Make sure any repairs

SEWING A FLAT-FELL SEAM

1 *Put the right sides of the cloth together and stitch a seam ½ inch from the edge.*

2 *Press the seam open, and trim one side of the seam allowance to half its width.*

3 *Fold the wider seam allowance over the trimmed edge and sew through all the layers. The resulting seam should always be on the back of the kite.*

will match the rest of the kite for strength. If a patch is applied to one side of a kite, it may affect the kite's stability, so keep the two sides symmetrical by applying a matching patch to the other side as well.

Kites made from paper or plastic can be repaired using cellophane tape or insulating tape. Fabric kites will often accept tape patches, too, or you can use spare pieces of fabric and glue or iron-on interfacing. Ripstop nylon kites can be repaired using special ripstop nylon tape or by sewing on a patch.

If a kite is damaged while flying, simple repairs can be made on the spot with tape, spare pieces of fabric, and glue or staples. It might be a good idea to carry a small emergency repair kit with you on flying expeditions just in case.

Remember, again, to keep the kite wings symmetrical.

MAKING A PATTERN

Where we have used a diagram for the basic parts of the kite, it will need to be scaled up to the finished size of the kite. You will need a large sheet of blank paper to make your pattern. Rule the paper into the same number of squares scaled up from the squares shown in the diagram – for example, 1-inch squares in the diagram, scaled up by 300% (written as "Scale: 1:3") will mean drawing squares of 3 inches on your pattern paper. Using erasable pencil, carefully copy the shape of the kite onto your pattern square by square. You should now have a full-size pattern to use in cutting out your material.

KNOTS

We recommend three types of knots – each has a different function:

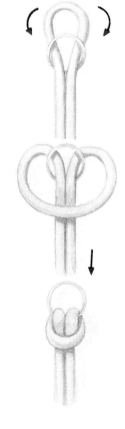

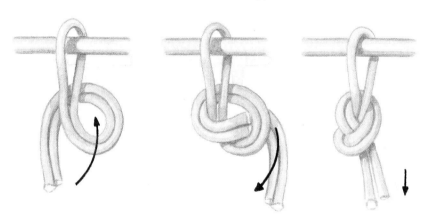

● **OVERHAND KNOT** makes a secure knot for attaching to split rings or around spars.

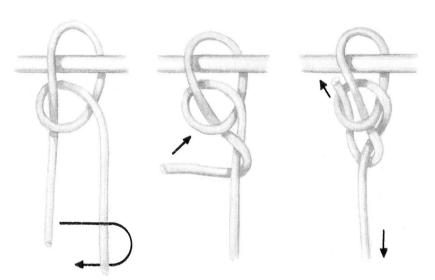

● **BOWLINE KNOT** is a non-slip knot for attaching lines to spars or handles.

● **LARK'S HEAD KNOT**
attaches a line to a ring, and can be slid up and down for adjustment e.g., for a towing point.

THE PROJECTS

SLED

DIFFICULTY: EASY   **WIND:** LIGHT – MEDIUM

The sled is a simple kite that is held in shape partly by spars that run along its length and partly by the pressure of the wind, which holds the kite open. The kite needs a long bridle to allow it to open fully. The sled shown here is patterned with what must be the most famous flag in the world, the Stars and Stripes. The same method may, of course, be used to create other flags or any other pattern you choose.

MATERIALS

Sheet plastic or strong plastic bag

Two ¼in. dowels, both 18in. long

Permanent marker pens

Cellophane tape

Strong thread

Metal ruler and craft knife or scissors

Sandpaper (optional)

22lb. breaking strain flying line

ALTERNATIVE MATERIALS

● **The kite can be made using reasonably strong but flexible paper for the sail. Nylon can also be used.**

ALTERNATIVE METHODS

● **You can make a scaled-down version of this kite using drinking straws as the spars. Such a kite will fly in light winds.**

● **Two tails may be attached, one to each of the bottom corners of the kite.**

● **Circular vents may be cut in the center panel of the kite to improve stability. Each hole should be 4in. in diameter. The center of each hole should be about** **4in. from the bottom edge of the kite and the same distance from the spars.**

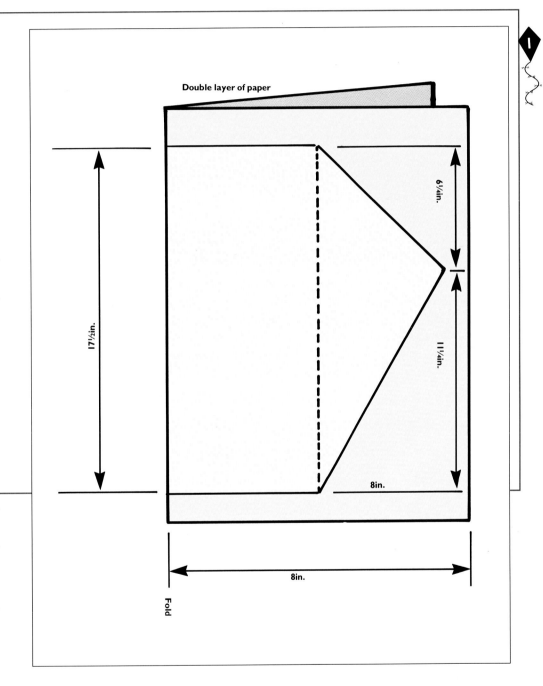

Double layer of paper

17½in.

6¼in.

11¼in.

8in.

8in.

Fold

I *Fold the plastic in half, then mark out the dimensions with a felt pen. Make sure that the center of the kite will be at the fold. Keeping the material* *folded, cut out the shape with a craft knife. Use a metal ruler to keep the cuts straight. (Alternatively, you can use a pair of scissors.)*

24

2 Unfold the plastic and decorate it with permanent-ink felt pens (water-based ink will smudge very easily). It may make decorating easier if you hold the plastic in place with tape, but you must be very careful not to damage the plastic when you remove the tape – test the tape on a spare piece of plastic first.

3 Cut the dowels to 18in. in length. Smooth the ends using sandpaper. Attach the dowels on the decorated side of the kite. Each should run from a top to a bottom corner as shown. The dowels are fixed in place with tape at intervals along their length. Reinforce the ends of the dowels with tape stuck over the dowels and around onto the back of the kite.

4 Reinforce the points of the fins with several layers of tape. Pierce holes in the reinforced parts for the bridle. Tie on a 6ft. bridle.

5 Tie a loop at the mid-point of the bridle to which to attach the line. Attach the flying line.

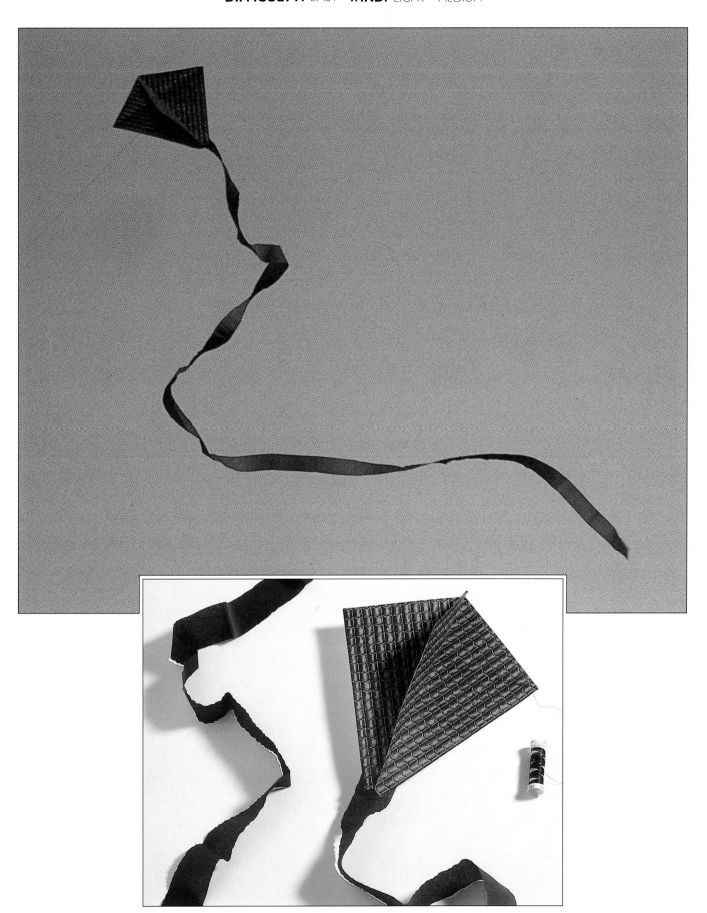

MATERIALS

Piece of wrapping paper
8¼in. × 11¾in.

10ft. length of crepe paper
for tail

9¼in. lightweight bamboo
spar (a bamboo kabob
skewer will do)

Cellophane tape

Glue stick

Craft knife or scissors

Metal ruler

Pencil

Button thread for flying
line

ALTERNATIVE MATERIALS

● This kite can be made
from any decorated
paper, provided it is not
too heavy.

● The bamboo spar could
be a piece from an old
bamboo shade or a split
garden cane.

● The spar could also be
made from balsa wood,
rattan cane, or even a
drinking straw.

● The pieces of kite can be
put together with staples
instead of glue.

26

A kite for beginners! A simple shape that is easy to make and easy to fly as long as the wind is not too strong. If the kite seems to fly erratically, try adding more length to the tail. If the wind gets too strong, the kite will be distorted and damaged, so stick to fairly calm days.

1 *Fold the paper in half with the pattern outward.*

2 *With the fold on your right, make a diagonal fold from a point ⅜in. in from the top left and bottom right corners, and fold the flap over. Turn the paper over and make a flap on the other side in the same way.*

3

4

5

6

3 *Open the paper out and, with the pattern facing you, line up a ruler with the wing tips. Mark the edge of the keel as shown.*

4 *Draw a line from the mark to the point at the bottom. Then fold out the lower flap so that it will not be damaged when you cut the keel. Now form the keel by cutting along the line you have drawn.*

5 *Glue the sides of the keel together.*

6 *Cut a short piece of spar to fit between the points of the wings. Attach the spar to the back of the kite with tape.*

7 Cut a strip of crepe paper 10ft. long and 1½in. wide. Stick one end of the strip onto the bottom of the kite with tape.

8 Make a hole in the keel, tie on the thread, and fly away!

SQUARE KITE

DIFFICULTY: INTERMEDIATE **WIND:** MEDIUM – QUITE STRONG

A test flight with this kite will establish whether you need to add length to the tail to improve stability. The angle of flight can also be changed to suit different wind conditions.

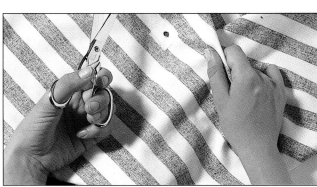

MATERIALS

Cotton fabric 23in. square

About 30ft. of 1½in. wide ribbon for tail

Four pieces of 1½in. wide ribbon, 19in. long (for decoration)

Iron-on interfacing, 1⅛in. square

1in. wide tape or grosgrain 16in. long

Two pieces of ¼in. dowel, 31in. long

Seven ½in. split rings

Strong thread

Scissors

Pencil or tailor's chalk

Strong braided line for bridles

44lb. flying line

ALTERNATIVE MATERIALS

● The dowel used could be a little thinner or thicker without affecting performance.

● The tails and decoration could be made of any scraps of cloth or crepe paper.

● This kite could be made from any cloth that is fairly dense and not liable to stretch too much. If you use a less porous cloth for this kite, you may need a stronger flying line.

● Although braided line is better for the bridles, you can use flying line instead.

1 *Find and mark the center of the square of fabric by first folding along one diagonal (from corner to corner), then folding the resulting triangle into equal halves so that the opposite corners meet as shown.*

2 *Cut a small piece of iron-on interfacing and iron it to the back of the fabric at the center point. Cut a small hole at the center; this will take one of the lines of the bridle, so it needs to be only about ¼in. in diameter. The edges can be finished with zigzag stitch if you wish.*

3 *Make a double-fold hem all around the edges of the kite to a depth of about ½in.*

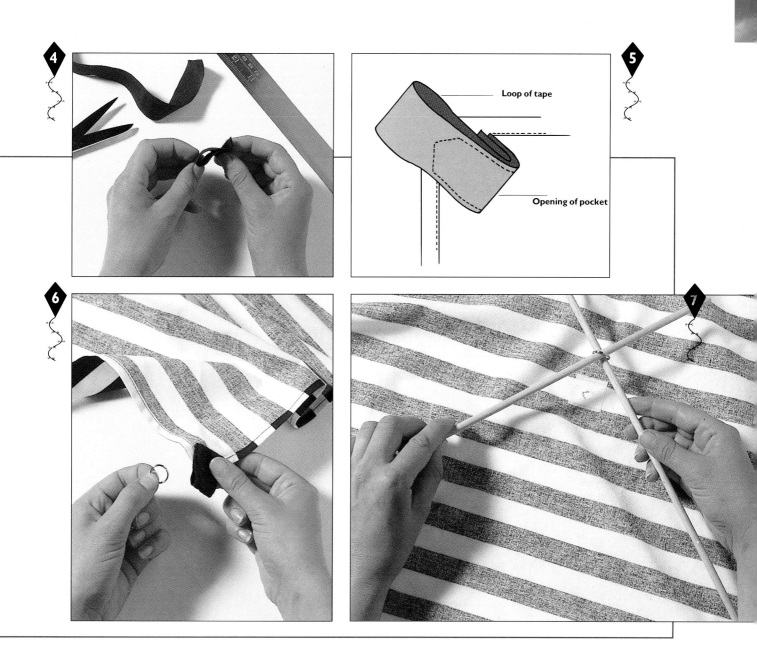

Loop of tape

Opening of pocket

4 To make the pockets, cut four pieces of 1in. wide tape to a length of 4in. each. Fold each piece in half and then fold over about 1in. of the loose ends together as shown.

5 Stitch the pockets to the back of the kite, placing one at each corner and leaving a loop of tape extending beyond the point to take a split ring, as shown in the diagram.

6 Thread a split ring onto each loop.

7 Cut two lengths of dowel about 31in. long. They should fit the kite snugly when they are placed crosswise from corner to corner. Smooth any rough ends with sandpaper. Fit the dowels into the pockets, threading them both through a split ring at the point where they cross.

8

Long bridle

Short bridle
(9¾in. long)

16¾in.

16¾in.

Front of kite

Ring

Ring

Long bridle

16¾in.

16¾in.

Loop

9

10

8 Make the bridles from three lengths of braided line, two pieces 35in. long and one 9¾in. long, each with a loop tied at both ends to thread onto the split rings. The two longer pieces also need a loop tied in the middle. From the front of the kite, attach the bridle as shown in the diagram.

9 Thread the unattached end of short line through the hole in the center of the kite and attach it to the split ring that joins the dowels.

10 To make the tail, fold the ribbon in half across its width and stitch a loop at one end. Thread the loop onto a split ring at the center of the bottom bridle. Decorate the kite with four short lengths of ribbon tied onto the split rings in the corners.

FIGHTER-STYLE KITE

DIFFICULTY: INTERMEDIATE   **WIND:** LIGHT

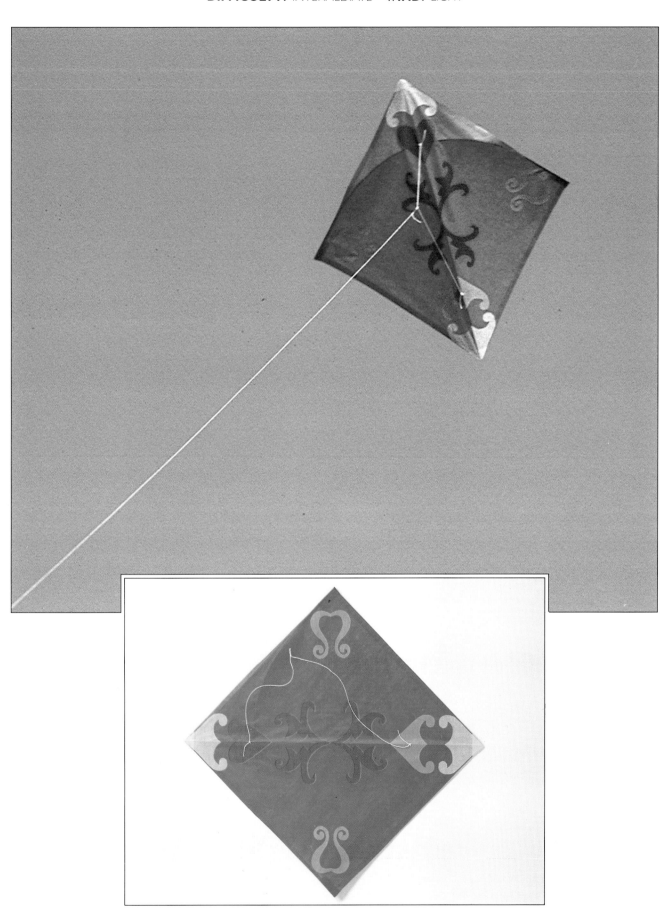

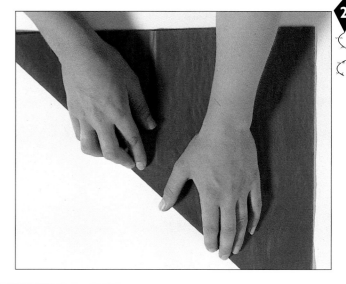

MATERIALS

Piece of tissue paper 16in. square

Pieces of tissue paper for decoration

⅛in. dowel, at least 21in. long

⅛in. cane, at least 24½in. long

Strong thread and a needle

Glue stick

Craft knife or junior hacksaw

Sandpaper

Scissors

Strong thread for flying line

ALTERNATIVE MATERIALS

● **The kite can also be made from wrapping paper or even newspaper!**

● **The spars are traditionally made from split bamboo, which could be taken from an old bamboo window shade.**

STEERING A FIGHTING KITE

Fighter kites are controlled by tightening and loosening the line. When the line is taut, the kite flies steadily. To turn the kite, let out some line and the kite will rotate in the air. When the kite is pointing in the direction you want, tighten the line again, and the kite will move in that direction. Steer the kite by holding the line, not the reel – leave the reel and some spare line lying on the ground (be careful not to trip on the loose line). You will need some practice before you become skilled at controlling your kite.

This kite, based on traditional Indian fighter kites, is light and well-balanced. It can be steered and performs best in a gentle breeze. The kite should not be flown in damp conditions because water will weaken or damage the tissue paper.

1 *Cut the tissue paper for the sail to make a 16in. square.*

2 *Fold the paper in half across the diagonal to mark the position of the spine and to make sure that both sides are the same size.*

3

4

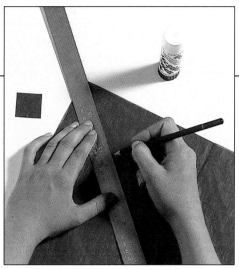

5

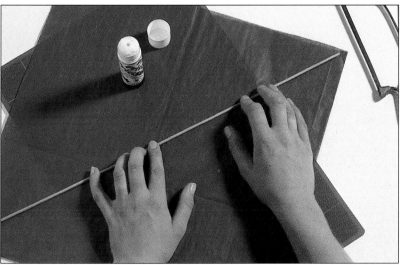

6

3 Decorate the front of the kite with cutout tissue paper shapes pasted in place with the glue stick. Make the pattern symmetrical to keep the weight even.

4 Mark two points, one 5⅜in. from each end of the fold on the back of the kite. Paste patches of tissue paper over the points with the glue stick as reinforcement.

5 Cut the dowel for the spine to 21in. long, and smooth any rough ends with sandpaper. Glue the dowel to the tissue paper at the fold, allowing an equal overlap of tissue paper at each end. Mark the positions of the tissue-reinforced points on the dowel.

6 Fold in and glue ⅜in. of paper along all the edges and over the tips of the spine top and bottom.

7 Cut the cane to 24½in. long and smooth the ends with sandpaper. Position one end of the cane in an empty corner of the paper, allowing enough overlap to fold over the cane. Glue the cane into the overlap securely.

8 Put a heavy weight on the glued corner, or get someone to hold it down securely. Bend the cane gently and fix the other end into the opposite corner in the same way as you fixed the cane in step 7. The cane should cross the spine at the point that you marked and reinforced earlier.

9 Glue reinforcing patches onto all four corners of the kite to give extra strength. Then cut a length of strong thread and thread the needle. Pierce the paper from front to back with the needle at the reinforced point where the spine and the spar cross. Wind the thread twice around the bowed cane. Return the thread through the paper on the other side of the spine.

10 Knot the thread on the front of the kite. Mark a place 10¼in. along the thread. Measure a further 12in. and mark the thread again. Pass the thread through the paper at the second reinforced point. Tie the thread around the spine at the second mark on the thread and cut off any extra. Find the first mark that you made on the thread, and tie a loop there to attach the flying line.

EDDY TRAIN

DIFFICULTY: INTERMEDIATE   **WIND:** MEDIUM – QUITE STRONG

MATERIALS

Brown wrapping paper 10ft. × 30in. (or four pieces at least 30in. square)

Eight pieces of ¼in. dowel, 28in. long

Cellophane tape

Acrylic paints, sponge, and plate for decoration

Strong glue

Scissors

Junior hacksaw

Crepe paper for tails

Strong thread or flying line

Water container in which to soak doweling (the bathtub will do)

88lb. flying line

ALTERNATIVE MATERIALS

● These kites can be made from any strong paper.

● The decoration can be done using any thick paint.

ALTERNATIVE METHODS

● Strong thread can be glued into the folded edges of each kite to give extra strength.

● The bridle point can be adjusted to suit different weather conditions.

FLYING TIPS

● In stronger winds these kites can pull surprisingly hard, so it is important to wear gloves made of leather (or some other strong material) to protect your hands from line burns.

● To launch the train, release the kites one at a time, starting with the one farthest from the flying line, and gradually feed them into the sky. It is extremely difficult to launch kite trains without assistance.

The Eddy Train described here consists of four kites strung together in a line. You can add more kites to the line as you become practiced in flying them – several will fly just as well as one. Obviously you will need a stronger flying line as the number of kites increases, and extra reinforcement on the vulnerable areas of the kites may be needed.

1 Cut the ¼in. dowel as necessary to make eight pieces 28in. long. Four of these dowels will be spines; make a mark 5¼in. from one end of each of these to indicate where the spars will intersect.

2 Make a slit in the other end of each spine to a depth of ¼in. (about the depth of a junior hacksaw blade). Be very careful with the saw – apply only gentle pressure and make sure that it does not slip and cut your hand.

The other four dowels will be cross-spars – mark the center of each. Make a similar slit in both ends of all four cross-spars, making sure that both the slits are made in the same plane.

3

4

5

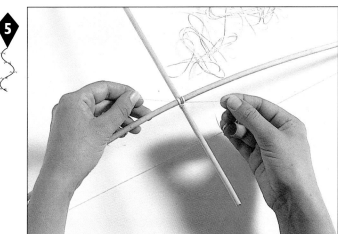

3 Soak the four cross-spars underwater for about two hours to make them more flexible.

Cut four 40in. lengths of strong line. Tie a knot near each end of all the pieces of line so that the knots are 26in. apart.

4 Slip the knoted line into the slit at one end of a soaked cross-spar. Bend the cross-spar carefully into a bow shape, and slip the knot at the other end of the line into the other slit. The distance between the line and the center of the bowed spar should be 3½in., and some adjustments may be necessary – check by measuring with a ruler.

Repeat the whole step with the other three cross-spars.

5 Join pairs of spines and cross-spars at the center marks by lashing the dowels together with strong line or thread and glue them for extra strength. Make sure that the two dowels are at right angles to each other with the bowed spar on top, as shown.

40

Fold

15½in.

29in.

27¼in.

Double layer of paper

Fold

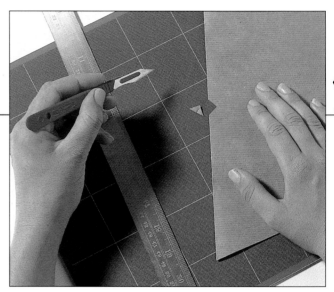

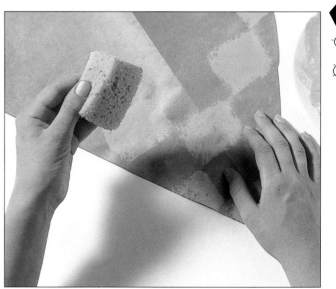

6 To make the sails, first fold the brown paper in half lengthwise. Cut out four pieces to the dimensions shown in the diagram.

7 Leave the paper folded, and cut out a small hole in each piece on the folded edge 5¾in. down from the top point.

8 Decorate the smooth side of the paper by printing a pattern with the sponge and paint (this step is, of course, optional).

9

10

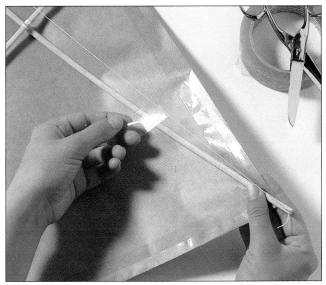

11

9 *Fold in ⅜in. of paper all around the edges toward the undecorated side, and trim off any excess on the corners. Anchor the folded edges all around with tape.*

10 *Position the dowels on the back of the kite, with the spine against the sail and the cross-spar above the spine. The top of the spine should be flush with the top point of the sail – all the other spar ends should extend slightly beyond the edge of the paper. Attach the dowels onto the paper at intervals with tape. Reinforce the points of the kite with extra tape.*

11 *When you have completed all four kites, join them together with strong line at the intersections of the spars. The kites should be about 6ft. apart. Knot the line at the intersection of the spars, thread through the hole in the sail, and measure the distance to the next kite. The patterned sides of the four kites should all face in the same direction.*

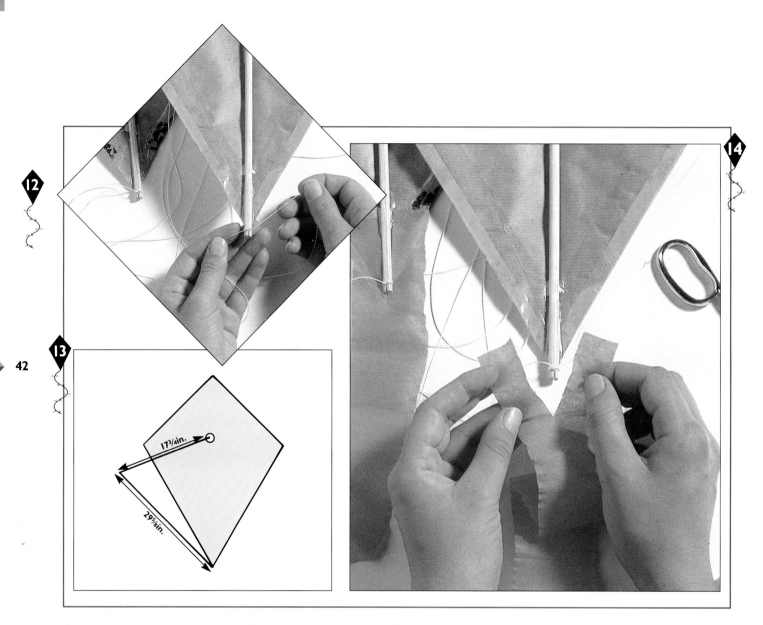

17³/₄in.

29⁵/₈in.

42

12 Join the kites together with a second line through the slit in the spar at the bottom of each kite. Tie the line around the stick and glue it for reinforcement. Make sure that the spacing of the kites remains even.

13 Make the front bridle as shown in the diagram.

14 Cut four pieces of crepe paper 3ft. long and 2in. wide for the tails. Snip a notch in the end of each piece and attach to the bottom of each kite with tape on each side of the spine.

D E L T A   B I R D

DIFFICULTY: INTERMEDIATE **WIND:** LIGHT – MEDIUM

MATERIALS

Black ripstop nylon 39in. wide

Scraps of colored ripstop nylon (for decoration)

Plastic tube to fit over dowels, 4¾in. long

¼in. dowel: two pieces 26in. long for wings and one piece 22½in. long for spine

½in. dowel: one piece 30in. long for spreader

Ruler

Glue stick

Scissors

Craft knife

Sandpaper

Strong thread

22lb. flying line

ALTERNATIVE MATERIALS

● **The dowel can vary in thickness slightly without affecting the performance of the kite.**

44

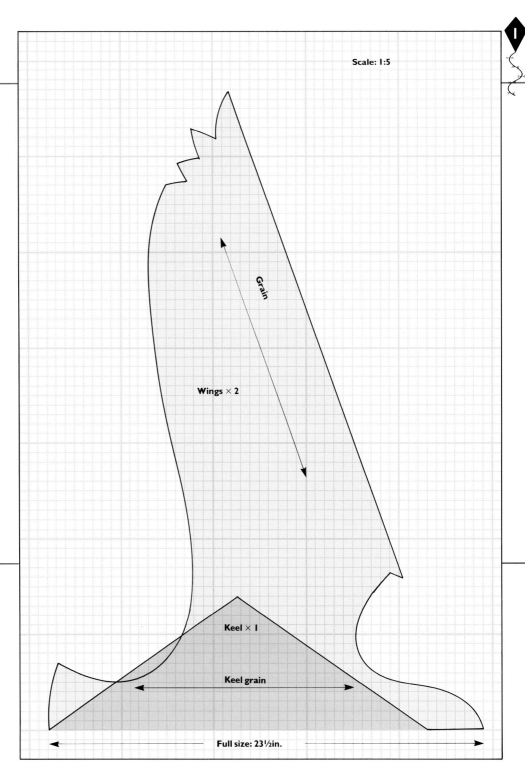

Scale: 1:5

Grain

Wings × 2

Keel × 1

Keel grain

Full size: 23½in.

The Delta Bird, as its name suggests, is very bird-like in flight – the kite will soar or hug the ground, and its wings flap. It is a very light-pulling kite, which requires a flying line of only 22lb.

1 *Using squared paper, scale up the drawing (see page 19), and make a plain paper template to the finished size.*

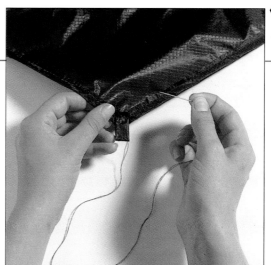

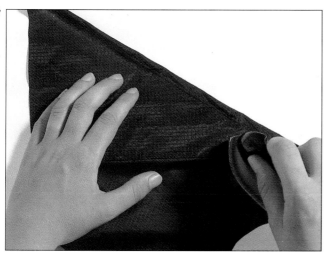

45

2 Fold the nylon and cut through both layers to produce two pieces to shape as shown. Pay careful attention to the direction of weave in the nylon, as marked on the template (step 1).

3 Hem the edge of the keel with a single fold ³⁄₈in. wide. Use a fairly long stitch – about four stitches per ½in. is best.

Cut a strip of nylon 2½in. long × 1½in. wide, fold the strip into three along its length and sew along the edges to form a narrow tab. Fold the tab in half across its width and sew it to the keel point to form a loop.

4 Place the wing pieces right (top) sides together, with the keel sandwiched between them in the position shown on the template. Now sew the wings and keel together, stitching through all three pieces ¼in. from the edge where they meet. Fold the wings back on each other (so that the keel is no longer between them), and press the seam out flat with a cool iron.

5 Sew a seam joining the wings (but this time not the keel) ¾in. in from the first line of stitching. Finish this seam ¾in. from the bottom of the wing and strengthen with backstitches. Leave space for the spine to be fed through and continue stitching down and across the bottom of the section. Fit the spine dowel into the casing, trimming the dowel if necessary. Decorate the wings and tail with pieces of nylon and attach with glue on the side with the keel.

6 Sew the sleeves for the wing spars on the back of the kite by making a ½in. hem along the fronts of the wings, using a single fold. Sew across the top and bottom, leaving a gap to insert the wing spars.

Mark and carefully cut out a hole for the spreader attachment in the seam on each wing, taking care not to cut through the stitching. See template for the exact position of the hole.

7 Cut two pieces of plastic tube, each 2½in. long. Using a craft knife, make two small cross-cuts in each piece; the cuts should be about a quarter of the way along each piece, on opposite sides.

8 Fit the wing dowels into the hems on the wings, threading them through the cross-cuts in the plastic tube. The tube should be at the center of the slot in the hem.

9 Fit the cross-spar into the plastic tubes across the back of the kite (the opposite side to the keel and decoration). The tubes will bend to give the wings some spring; in flight the wings will appear to flap. Tie the flying line onto the loop on the keel.

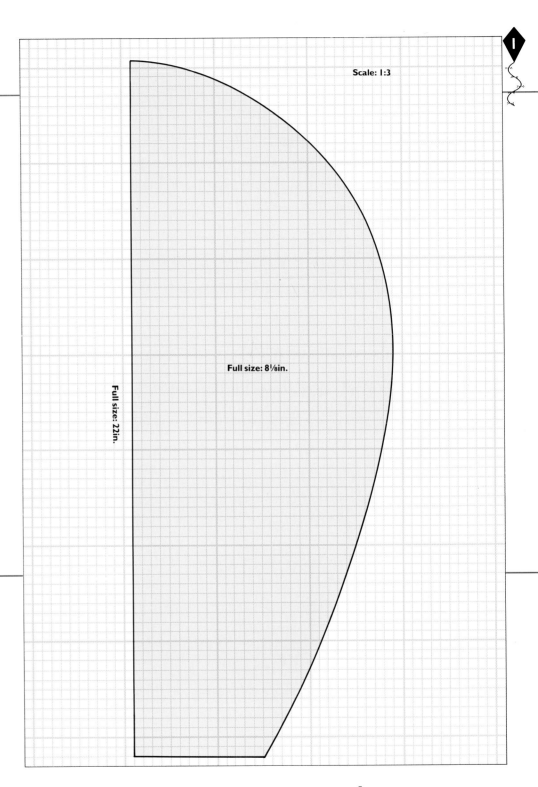

Scale: 1:3

Full size: 8⅛in.

Full size: 22in.

MATERIALS

Two pieces of paper – like typing paper, 23⅜in. × 16½in.

Crepe paper of one color, 20ft. long, for tail

Crepe paper of a second color for decoration

Various colored paper for decoration

60in. of ¼in. cane

20in. of ¼in. dowel

Strong thread

Cellophane tape

Glue stick

Permanent felt pen

Pencil

Scissors

Junior hacksaw

22lb. flying line

ALTERNATIVE MATERIALS

● **This kite can be made using any lightweight paper or plastic.**

● **Bamboo sticks may be used for the spars.**

● **The colors of the sail and tail materials may, of course, be varied.**

The serpent shape of this kite makes it great fun to fly – it is especially enjoyed by children. If the kite is going to be flown in heavier winds, it may be necessary to add length to the tail in order to improve its stability.

I *Copy the head template onto a folded piece of paper, scaling it up to full size (see page 19) and cut out the shape.*

2 Put the pattern onto a sheet of kite paper that has been folded in half. The straight edge of the pattern sheet must align along the fold in the kite paper.

Using a pencil, draw around the pattern for the head on the folded kite paper. Cut with a pair of scissors along the line you have drawn.

3 On the back of the kite, mark the two points at which you will attach the bridle. Both points should be on the fold line down the middle of the kite. One point should be 4½in. from the top (curved edge) of the kite, the other 2½in. from the bottom (straight edge). Reinforce these points using tape or by gluing on patches of paper.

4 Decorate the face of the kite using colored markers and patches of colored paper. Cut paper shapes with scissors and glue them on using a glue stick. A symmetrical pattern is best and, when paper is used, will not unbalance the kite. The easiest way to achieve symmetrical patterns is to cut them from paper folded in two.

5 Cut a length of cane 49in. long (the short remaining piece will be needed later). Smooth the ends with sandpaper. Mark the center of the cane.

50

6 *Mark three points on the kite: one ¾in. from the top on the center line; one in the bottom right corner, ¾in. from the edges; one in the bottom left corner, ¾in. from the edges.*

7 *Using tape, anchor the center of the cane to the point you have marked at the top of the kite.*

8 *Bend the cane and attach the ends to the points you have marked in the bottom corners, again using tape. Then use tape to attach the other parts of the cane to the paper.*

9 *Cut the shorter piece of cane so that it will fit between the ends of the curved cane. Then place it in position so that it is touching at both ends, and attach it with tape.*

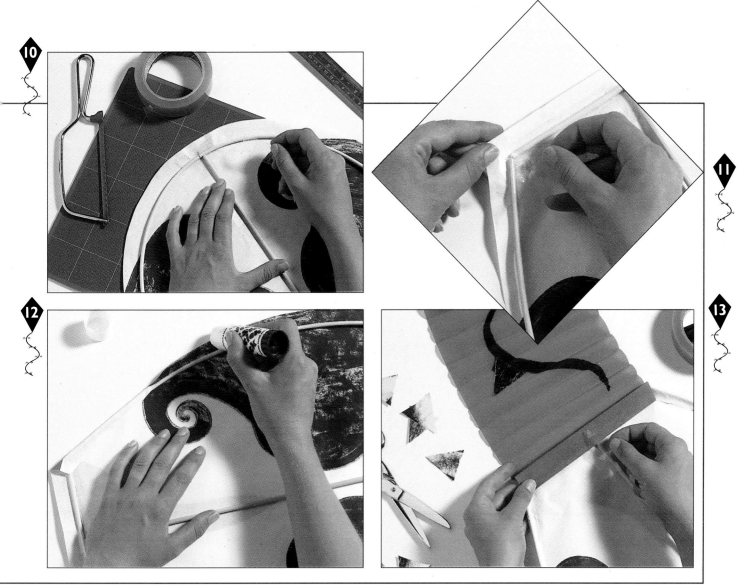

10 *Using a hacksaw, cut the dowel to make the spine, which will run from the curved cane to the straight cane along the center line of the kite. The dowel will need to be approximately 19⅝in. long. Once it is cut to the correct length, anchor the spine dowel in place with tape.*

11 *Using the tape, reinforce the joints between all the spars.*

12 *Fold the kite paper over the spars all around the edge and glue them in place using the glue stick.*

13 *To make the tail, first cut a crepe-paper strip the same width as the bottom of the kite and 20ft. long. Decorate it with felt pens and pieces of colored paper. Attach this main part of the tail to the kite with tape.*

14

15

16

17

14 Make six fin shapes of a contrasting color. To do this, fold some crepe paper into six and cut out the shape. Stick three of the fins onto each side of the tail.

15 Make a tassel by first cutting a strip of crepe paper about 20in. wide and 4in. deep. Then fold the paper along its length and, holding one end, snip to within ½in. of the edge of the paper with scissors.

16 Cut a strip of a different color, the same width as the main strip at one end and tapering to a point at the other. Glue the wide end to the bottom end of the tail. Attach the tassel to the point with tape.

17 Fix the bridle to the kite. The bridle, which should be 6ft. long, is tied around the spine dowel at the points you marked in step 3.

To find the point for the flying line to be attached, hold the bridle over your finger; when the wind lifts the kite to the appropriate angle, tie a loop in the bridle and fix the flying line to this. You should use line with at least 22lb. breaking strain.

PROJECT 8

DIAMOND STUNTER

DIFFICULTY: INTERMEDIATE   **WIND:** QUITE STRONG

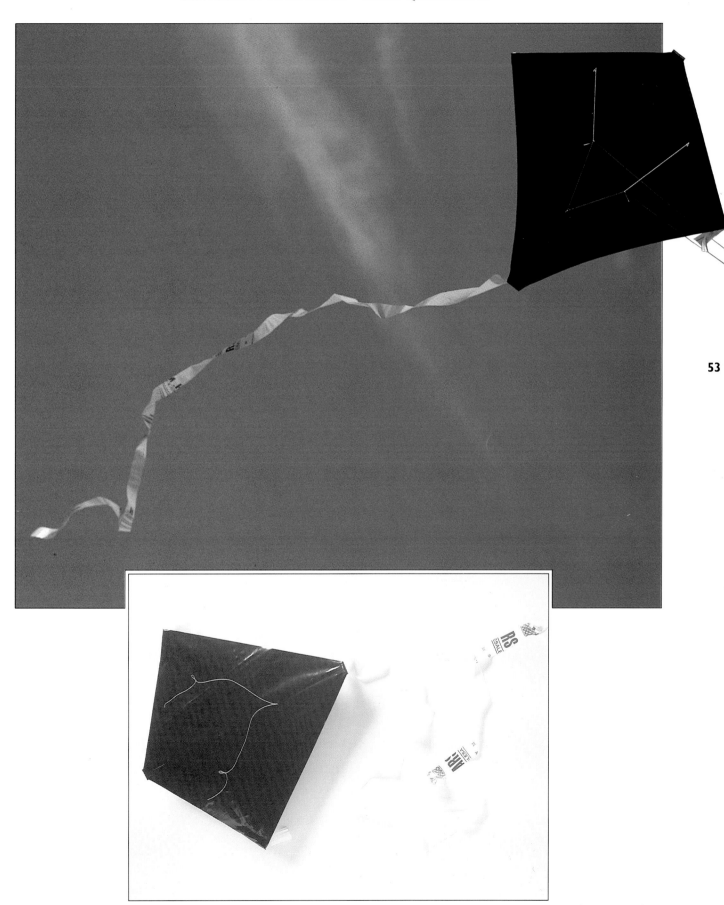

53

DIFFICULTY: INTERMEDIATE   **WIND:** QUITE STRONG

This kite will perform gracefully once the flying technique has been mastered. The flying lines must be exactly the same length; once the kite is airborne, pulling on both lines will cause the kite to rise and using the left and right lines will produce sideways movement. With a little practice, the diamond stunter is great fun to fly and to watch.

MATERIALS

Strong sheet of plastic or a garbage bag

Colorful plastic shopping bag for decoration and tail

⅛in. fiberglass rod, 35in. long

⅛in. fiberglass rod, 33in. long

⅛-¼in. reinforced plastic tube, 2in. long

Cellophane tape

Masking tape or insulating tape

Craft knife or scissors

Hacksaw

Ruler

Permanent marker pen

Sandpaper

6ft. strong line for bridle

Two 22lb. flying lines with handles

ALTERNATIVE MATERIALS

● **This kite can be made from almost any non-stretch plastic.**

ALTERNATIVE METHODS

● **Removing the tail will make this kite even more responsive.**

● **If more robust materials are used, this kite can be bounced off the ground and will continue to fly.**

● **The lighter the kite is, the less wind it will need to fly successfully.**

54

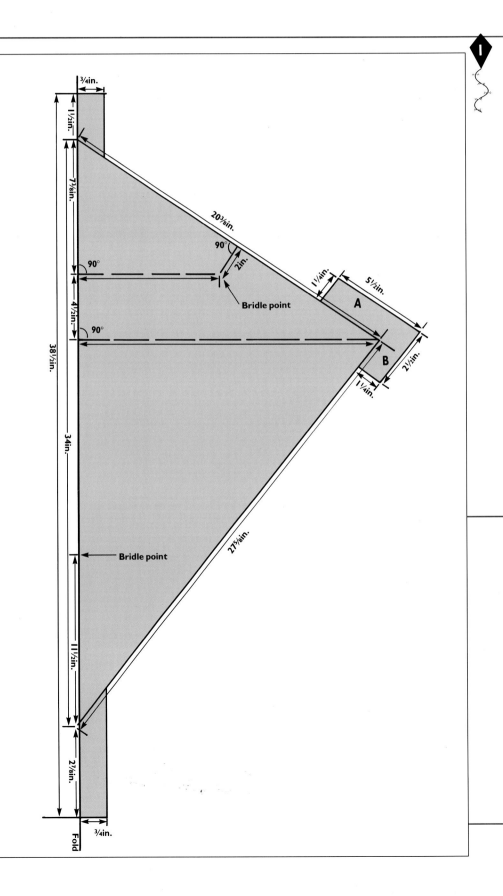

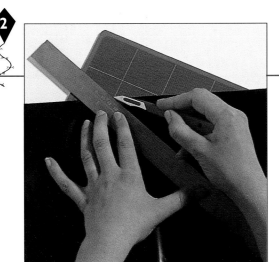

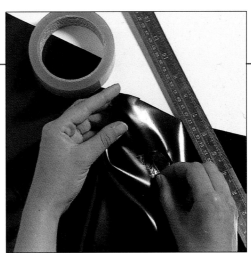

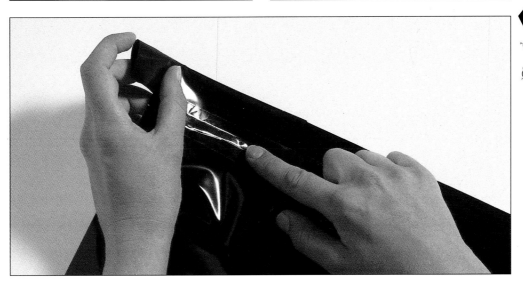

55

1 Fold the plastic in half and use a permanent felt pen to mark the shape to the dimensions shown. Make sure the center of the kite falls on the fold.

2 Keep the plastic folded, and cut out the shape using a sharp craft knife or scissors.

3 Unfold the plastic and mark the bridle points (see diagram). Reinforce the areas with tape and pierce a hole in each.

4 To make the corner pockets, fold flap A (see diagram) over and secure with tape, then fold flap B over, stick down and reinforce with tape. Repeat on the other corner of the kite.

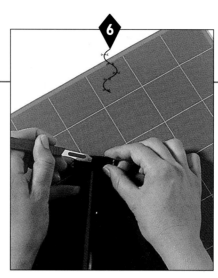

5 Cut two pieces of reinforced plastic tube 1 in. long. Attach one piece of these to the tab at the bottom of the kite with tape.

6 Roll the tube up in the tab. Make a cross-cut through the plastic and the tube with a sharp craft knife. This is to take the ⅛in. fiberglass rod that will make the spine and must be a tight fit, so it is better to make the cuts too small and enlarge them later if necessary.

7 Roll the tube over so that the cross-cut faces the top of the kite. Anchor the tube into place with tape and reinforce well.

Now repeat steps 6 and 7 on the top of the kite, but this time finishing with the cross-cut facing down.

8 Using a hacksaw, cut a length of ⅛in. fiberglass rod to fit tightly between the top and bottom of the kite. This will be 33in. long. Smooth the ends with sandpaper. Position the rod between the top and bottom tubes, making sure the ends fit snugly into the cross-cuts. Remove the spine again.

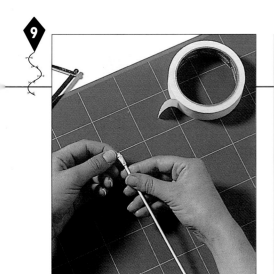

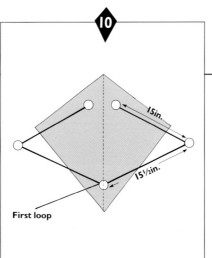

15in.

15½in.

First loop

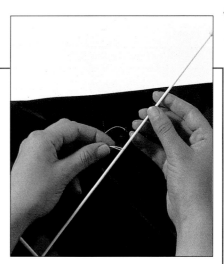

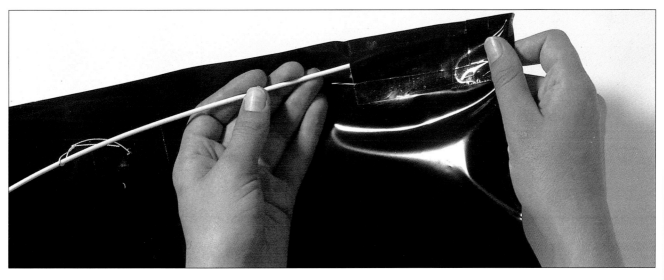

9 To make the cross-spar, cut a piece of ⅛in. fiberglass rod about 35in. long. Check before cutting that the spar will cross both bridle points; in order to do this, it will have to bow slightly. Smooth any sharp ends and wrap them with a length of masking tape, folding the tape over the end to prevent the spar from piercing the sail.

10 To make the bridle, first make a loop in the middle of 6ft. of line. Then make further loops in the positions shown in the diagram. The dimensions must be exactly the same on both sides of the kite.

11 To fix the bridle to the kite, thread the loops through the sail onto the spine and cross-spar.

12 Fix the spine and the cross-spar into position, with the cross-spar on top of the spine. The cross-spar will need to bow to fit into the corner pockets.

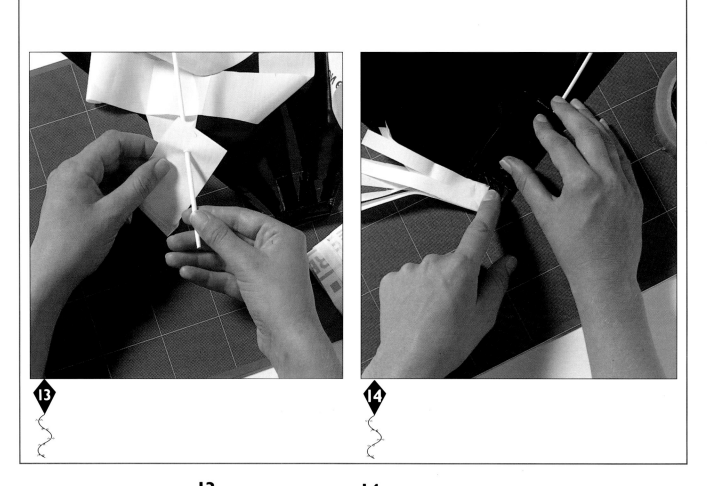

13 *To make the tail, cut a plastic shopping bag into 2in. strips and stick them together, end to end, to make a length of about 18ft. Reinforce the end of the tail with tape, pierce a hole, and thread it onto the spine (you will have to remove the spine from its socket to do this).*

14 *Stick a short piece of plastic bag, folded once or twice and cut with scissors to make a fringe, onto each corner of the kite for decoration.*
Tie on two flying lines of 22lb. breaking strain to the bridle.

D E L T A   S T U N T E R

DIFFICULTY: MORE ADVANCED   **WIND:** MEDIUM – QUITE STRONG

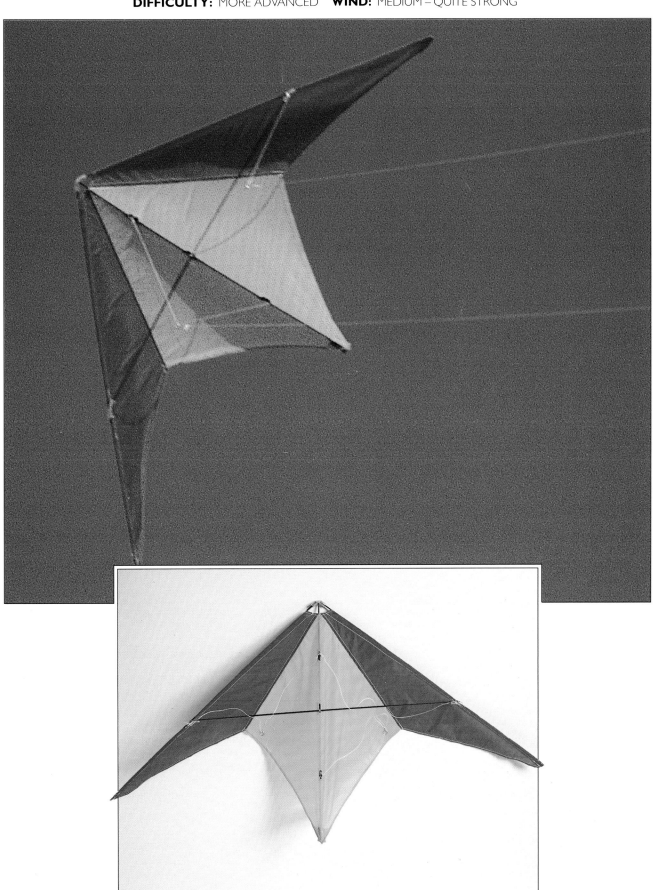

This kite can perform some spectacular stunts once you have mastered the flying technique, but do not practice in a crowded place, for safety reasons. The kite can be quite noisy when flown in stronger wind conditions. Small adjustments to the bridle may be necessary for effective flying.

MATERIALS

Red ripstop nylon 39in. square

Green ripstop nylon 39in. × 20in.

⅛in. carbon fiber rod: two pieces 36in. long, one piece 30in. long and one piece 33in. long.

Reinforced plastic tube 5in. long

Two ⅝in. split rings

Two rubber faucet washers (to fit spine)

Strong braided line for bridles

Cellophane tape

Double-sided tape

Extra strong thread

Insulating tape

Rubber band

Scissors

Craft knife

Junior hacksaw

88lb. flying line and two handles

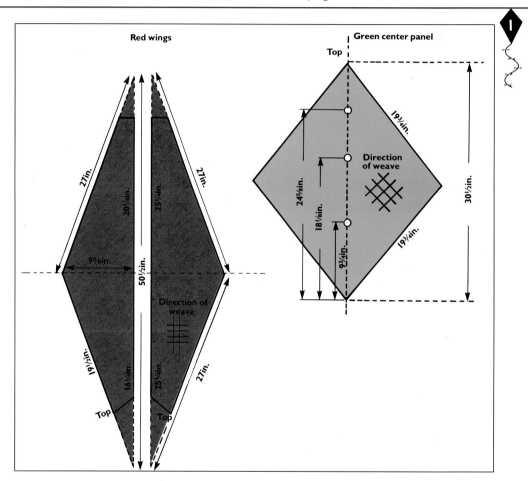

ALTERNATIVE MATERIALS

● The carbon fiber rod can be replaced with a fiberglass rod or dowel, although the resulting kite will be less responsive. It is important that the spreader is fairly rigid.

I *Cut the wings from the red nylon and the center panel from the green nylon to the dimensions shown – be sure to note the direction of the fabric grain in each case.*

2

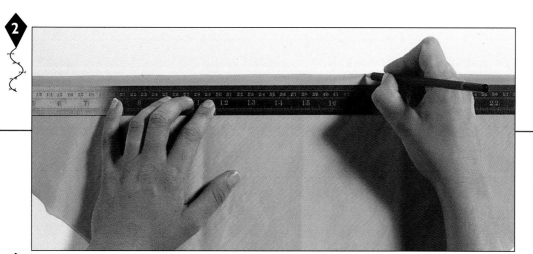

3

4

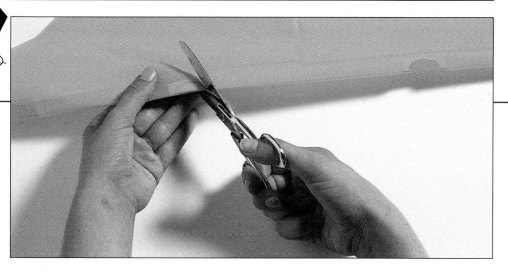

2 *Fold the center panel in half and mark the positions of the holes along the fold (see diagram to step 1). The holes will take the bridles when the kite is finished.*

3 *To reinforce the holes, stick a piece of double sided tape onto a spare piece of nylon 1½in. long. Peel off the backing and stick it onto the back of the panel over the hole positions.*

4 *Cut out the holes carefully with the panel folded in half.*

62

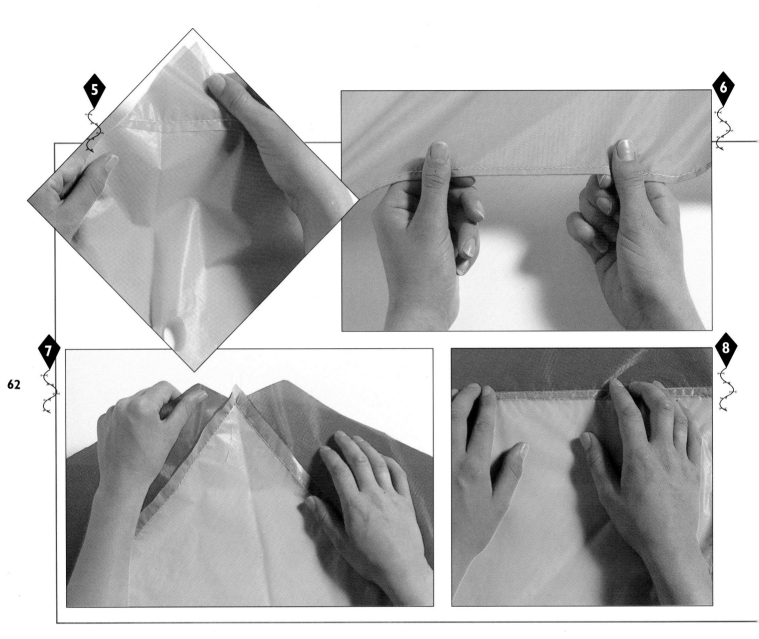

5 *Sew a triangular reinforcement of green nylon to the back of the kite in the bottom corner of the center panel.*

6 *Make a double fold hem of ½in. along the bottom edge of the center panel. Make sure the hem falls on the back of the kite, and use a long stitch – about three stitches to ½in. Make a similar hem along the bottom edges of the red side panels.*

7 *Join the red side panels to the center green panel with a ½in. seam on the back of the kite. The seams should end just short of the top of the kite.*

8 *Fold the seam allowance over onto the red wing, and sew through all the layers onto the wing to make a neat flat seam as shown.*

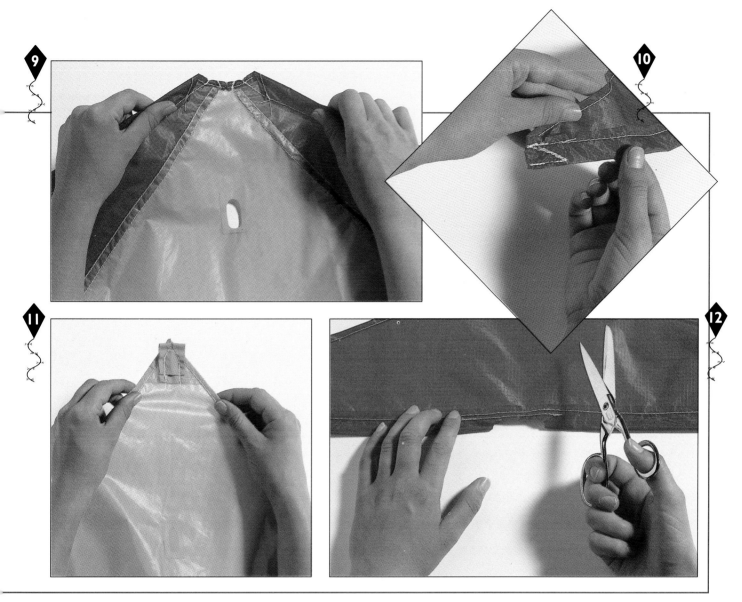

9 *Finish the seams and trim off any excess fabric. Fold ¼in. of fabric over onto the back of the kite and stitch securely around the top of the kite. Fold in the side spar casing by ¾in. and stitch near the edge.*

10 *Fold in the wing tip by ½in. Turn the tips over once more by about 1⅛in. and sew along the edges to form a pocket for the spars.*

11 *Cut a piece of nylon 13in. long × 1⅛in. wide to make the bottom pocket. Fold the strip in half and in half again, and stitch to the back of the kite as shown.*

12 *Make a semicircular cut in each wing to accept the plastic tube for the cross-spar. Each cutout should be about 2in. long, and they must be symmetrical. The center of the cutout should be 14½in. from the bottom wing tip. Reinforce the cutouts with another row of stitching.*

13 Cut two pieces of reinforced plastic tube 1 ½in. long. Slice a V-shaped notch in the center of each piece of tube with a craft knife as shown. These will fit onto the wing spars to take the spreader.

14 Cut a third piece of plastic tube 2in. long and make a cross-cut in one side. This will be for the nose of the kite.

15 Using a hacksaw, cut two wing spars 36in. long from the carbon fiber rod. Wrap some insulating tape around one end of each spar so that they will fit the plastic nose tube tightly.

16 Wrap some tape around each spar with the edge of the tape 14in. from the untaped end.

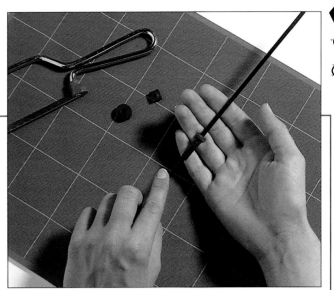

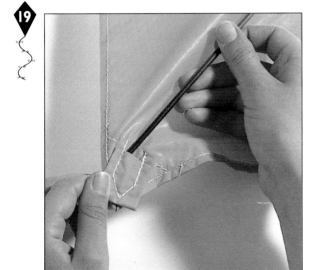

65

17 *Feed the wing spar through the sleeve on the wing from the top of the kite. The spar should pass through the plastic cross-spar connector at the cutout in the hem and down to the wing tip. The tape wrapping on the spar will fit inside the tube when the spar is in position.*

18 *From the carbon fiber rod, cut a piece 30in. long for the spine. Wrap a strong rubber band around the middle of the spine. Wrap the spine with tape at the top and bottom, so that the edge of the tape is 6½in. from the top and 8½in. from the bottom. Trim the faucet washers square and fit one onto each end of the spine outside the two taped places.*

19 *Fit the bottom of the spine into the bottom pocket of the kite, and the top into the cross-cut of the plastic nose tube.*

20 *Fit the wing spars into the nose tube, making sure that they fit tightly. Bending the nose tube down when you fit the spars will help to grip the spine.*

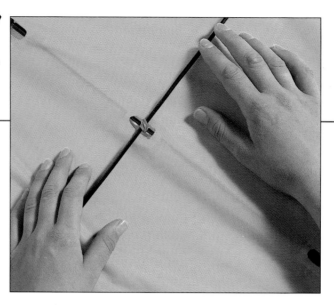

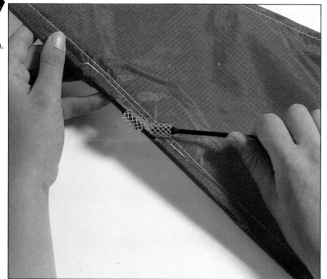

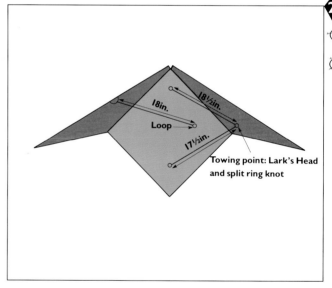

Loop

18in.

18½in.

17½in.

Towing point: Lark's Head
and split ring knot

21 *From the carbon fiber rod, cut a piece 33in. long for the spreader. Mark the center point. With the spreader on the top of the kite, thread the spreader through the rubber band on the spine up to the center mark.*

22 *Wrap the ends of the spreader with insulating tape. Then fit the ends of the spreader into the tubes fixed to the wing spars. Make sure they fit tightly, adding more tape wrapping if necessary.*

23 *Make two bridles, each of which has three legs. The diagram shows the construction of one of the bridles – the other should be a "mirror image" on the other side of the kite. You will need two pieces of line for each bridle. Note that the measurements given are for the finished bridle, after the knots have been tied. It's a good idea to mark the line*

clearly with a felt tip at the towing point. Attach a split ring to the towing point using a lark's head knot, before threading the loop of the outer leg onto the ring. When you have made both bridles, attach one flying line to each of the split rings.

To fine-tune the kite, move the towing point slightly by loosening and adjusting the lark's head knot.

BOX KITE

DIFFICULTY: INTERMEDIATE   **WIND:** MEDIUM – QUITE STRONG

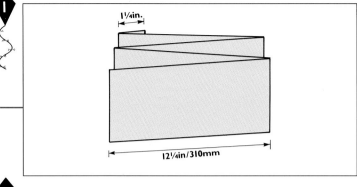

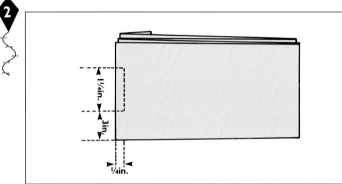

MATERIALS

Two strips of brown
  wrapping paper 50in. ×
  7in.

Four pieces of ¼in. dowel,
  27in. long

Four pieces of ¼in. dowel,
  16½in. long

Plastic tube to fit over
  dowel, 9½in. long

Cellophane tape

Marker pens

Craft knife

Junior hacksaw

Scissors

33lb. flying line

ALTERNATIVE MATERIALS

● The box kite can be made
  from any type of strong
  paper.

● The thickness of the
  dowel and plastic tube
  can vary slightly if
  necessary.

The box design of this kite gives it rigidity and strength, and the kite will be stable in flight even in quite strong wind conditions. Brown wrapping paper may seem an unassuming material to use, but it is surprisingly strong. At the end of a flying session, if great care is taken, the box kite can be collapsed down flat to make it easier to carry home.

1 *Cut out two strips of paper 50in. × 7in. Fold the strips of paper as shown.*

2 *Measure and mark with a pencil the position for holes on both of the folded edges. Make each hole 1 ⅛in. wide and ¼in. deep centered on the width of the paper. Unfold the paper and reinforce the places where holes will be cut using tape on the back of the paper.*

3 *Fold the paper again and cut out the holes through all the thicknesses – you will be cutting more than one hole at once.*

4 Decorate the front of the paper strips with marker pens.

5 Cut four lengths of dowel 27in. long. Smooth any rough ends with sandpaper. Measure and mark each piece of dowel ⅜in. and 4¼in. from both ends. These marks will serve to position the tubes that hold the cross-spars.

6 Cut eight pieces of plastic tube 1⅛in. long using the hacksaw. Slit each piece at the center, taking care not to cut completely through the tube.

7 Slide a piece of tube onto each end of each doweling spar. The spars should pass into the end of the tube and exit through the slit you made in step 6. Line up the end of each tube with one of the marks on a spar. Make sure that both spurs of the tubes on each spar face in the same direction.

70

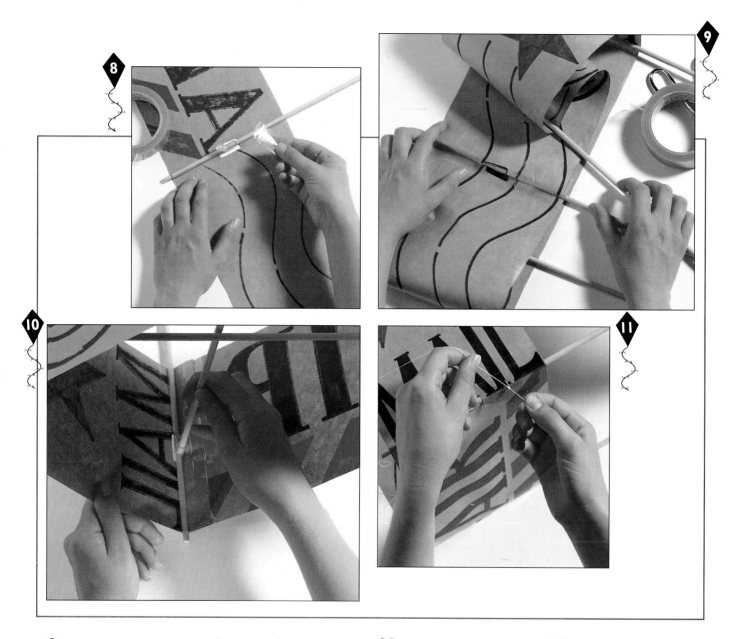

8 Lay the spars onto the inside of one of the strips of the brown paper, aligning each spar with a fold. The spars should extend ⅜in. beyond the edge of the paper and the tubes should be pointing up. Using tape, fix the spars securely onto the paper.

Repeat with the other strip of paper, attaching it to the other ends of spars in the same way.

9 Join the edges of both paper strips with tape back and front, so that each forms a complete "band." The 1⅛in. of paper in step 1 allows for an overlap.

10 Cut four dowels to make cross-spars 16½in. long. Smooth rough ends with sandpaper. Fit the cross-spars into the internal plastic tubes to brace the box. Take great care, as the paper is most liable to tear at this stage. The spars must be a good fit – if they are at all loose, wind some tape around them; if they are too long, shorten them slightly until they fit. Reinforce all the joints between spars and paper with tape.

11 The flying line is tied directly onto the kite (no bridle is used). Pierce two small holes 5¾in. down from the end of a corner spar, one on each side of the spar. Thread the flying line through one hold, around the spar, back through the other hole, and tie securely. Reinforce with tape.

This colorful kite is fun to fly, but will pull quite strongly even in moderate wind conditions – use a strong flying line and wear protective gloves to avoid line burns.

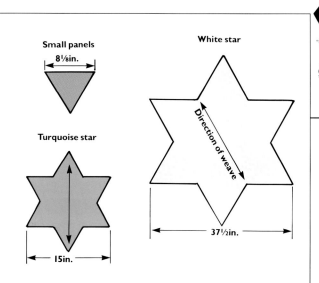

MATERIALS

Plain white paper for templates

39in. wide ripstop nylon in four colors: 4ft. of white, 3ft. of turquoise, 3ft. of purple; and 2ft. 6in. of green

Seven ¼in. split rings

Three pieces of ⅜in. dowel, each 3ft. long

33ft. of strong fabric tape ½in. wide

Strong thread or buttonhole thread and needle

Scissors

Junior hacksaw

Glue stick

Strong braided line for bridles

88lb. flying line

ALTERNATIVE MATERIALS

- This kite can be made more simply by cutting out a hexagon shape instead of a star. Simply join the points of the star on the template with straight lines. The bridling remains the same.

- The kite can be made in one color only, without the appliqué.

72

Small panels
8⅛in.

Turquoise star

White star

Direction of weave

37½in.

15in.

1 Draw the pattern onto plain paper and cut out. All the pieces are based on equilateral triangles. Fold the white nylon in half and use the pattern to cut out the star shape, noting the direction of the fabric grain. Mark the center of the star. Cut out the turquoise star and mark the center.

2 Cut out the triangular decorative panels using the relevant patterns and colors. There are three green and three purple panels. The grain of each piece must match the grain of the white base. Glue the panels into position in the points of the star using glue stick around the edges. Glue the turquoise star into position, lining up the center marks.

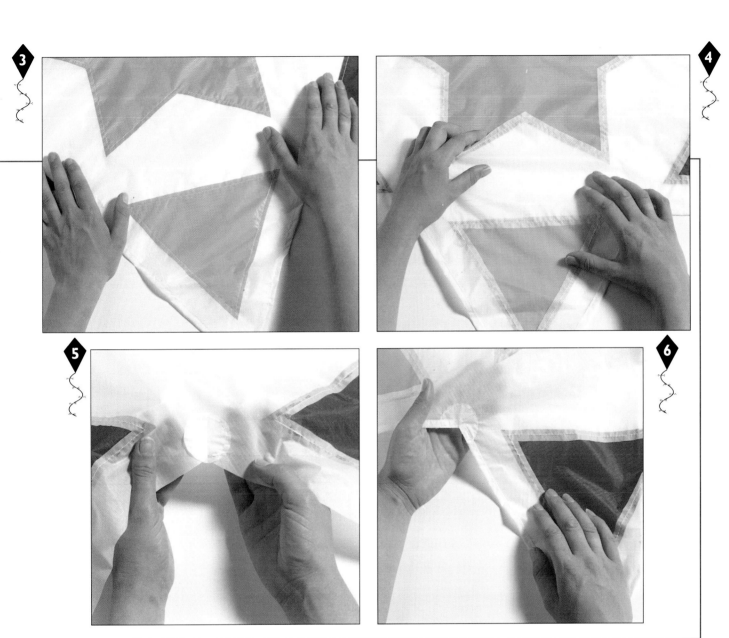

3 Stitch the colored panels into place using a long stitch (about three stitches per ½in.). Sew ¼in. in from the edge of the panel, onto the front of the kite.

4 On the back of the kite, cut away the white base behind each colored panel ¼in. in from the line of stitching.

5 Cut six circles of nylon about 1¾in. in diameter. Stitch the circles onto the back of the kite between the points as shown to act as reinforcement. Make a slit through both the reinforcement and the kite to the depth of the seam allowance, extending to the center of the circle. This will make it easier to turn a hem at this point.

6 Double fold a hem ½in. deep all around the edges of the white star, and trim off any excess fabric at the points. Sew a double row of stitches over each circular patch to reinforce the edges.

74

7 Cut a strip of turquoise nylon 6¼in. long × 1½in. wide. Fold the strip in half lengthwise, and then in half again. Sew it onto the center of the back of the kite, using double rows of stitching.

To make the center back tie, cut a strip of white nylon 20in. long × 1½in. wide. Fold the strip into thirds along its length and sew along the edge. Sew the tie onto the back of the kite using double rows of stitching.

8 To make the loops for the split rings, cut four strips of white nylon approximately 2¾in. long × 1½in. wide, and one strip of turquoise nylon to the same size. Fold each strip into thirds along its length and sew along the edge. Sew a white loop onto four points of the star, choosing two opposing pairs of points.

9 Sew the turquoise loop made in step 8 onto the center front of the kite using double rows of stitching. Thread a split ring onto all four white loops and the turquoise loop.

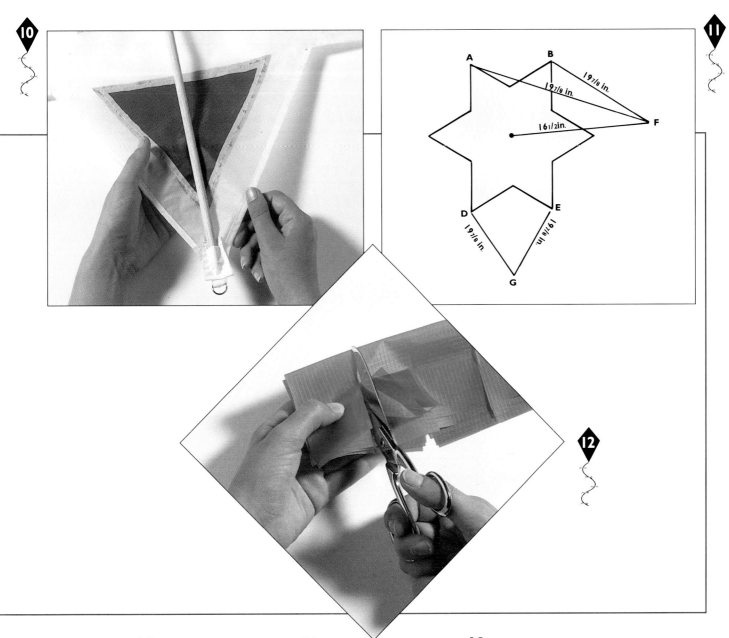

Diagram labels: A, B, D, E, F, G; 19⅞ in., 19⅞ in., 16½ in., 19⅞ in., 19⅞ in.

10 To make the star pockets, cut six strips of white nylon, 13in. long × 1⅛in. wide. Fold each strip in half and in half again, then double over and sew into place on each point of the star at the back of the kite using a double row of stitching around the edge. These pockets will take the ends of the spars when the kite is complete.

11 Fix the bridle as shown in the diagram. A to B and D to E is a continuous length of braided line. Remember to allow extra for the take up on the loop. Thread split rings onto the loops at F and G. Check that the kite is evenly balanced by holding it at F.

12 For the tail, cut 10 different colored strips of nylon 3ft. long × 6in. wide. Fold the strips in half along their length, then into four across their width and snip along the unfolded side to make a fringe. Make each cut about 2in. deep, and about 2in. apart.

13 *Stitch the fringed strips along the center onto a length of fabric tape, overlapping each color slightly at the joins.*

14 *Sew a loop at one end of the tape and fix the tail to the split ring at G (see diagram for step 11).*

15 *Cut three pieces of ⅜in. dowel to about 3ft. long. Round off the ends with sandpaper.*

16 *Fit the dowels across the star into the pockets. They should be a snug fit. The horizontal dowel will be especially tight as there is less stretch here on the grain of the fabric. Tie the dowels together with the white nylon tie.*

KEELED DIAMOND

DIFFICULTY: MORE ADVANCED **WIND:** MEDIUM – QUITE STRONG

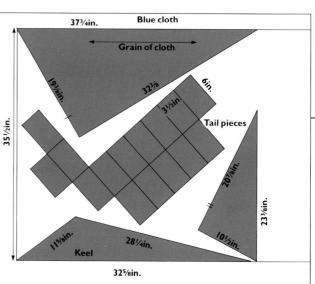

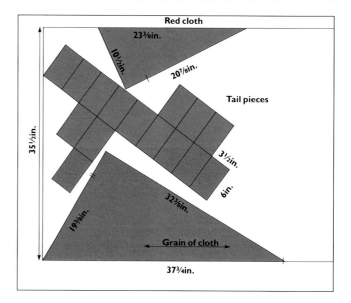

MATERIALS

Blue cotton poplin 35in. wide × 3ft.

Red cotton poplin the same size

⅜in. dowel, 6ft. long

½in. wide tape, 18ft. long

1¼in. grosgrain ribbon (or wide tape), 18in. long

Strong thread and needles

Two ¼in. eyelets and a punch (or equivalent) for fixing (optional)

Fishing swivel clip (optional)

Junior hacksaw

Scissors

Sandpaper

Pencil or tailor's chalk

44lb. flying line

ALTERNATIVE MATERIALS

● The sail can be made from any densely woven cloth that is not liable to stretch too much like sheeting or lining.

● Thinner dowel can be used if necessary.

● The pockets can be made of any thick fabric tape.

● Tape loops can be used instead of the eyelets.

ALTERNATIVE METHODS

● Although a flat-fell seam is recommended for neatness and strength, you can simply stitch the cloth together leaving the raw edges at the back of the kite. The more rows of stitching you use, the less the kite will stretch. Another alternative is to stitch fabric tape over the seams.

This two-tone kite with its tail of bows is very traditional in shape. The length of the kite's tail will need to vary depending on the wind conditions; stronger winds need a longer tail. The flying line can also be moved from the top eyelet (for light winds) to the lower one (for stronger winds).

I *Make paper templates for each color as shown in the diagrams. Place the templates on the right color cloth, making sure the direction of the weave is correct. Mark the outlines in pencil or tailor's chalk and cut out carefully. You will have two red and two blue triangles for the kite body, and a narrow blue triangle for the keel.*

2

3

4

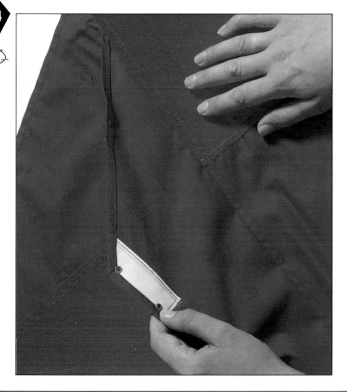

5

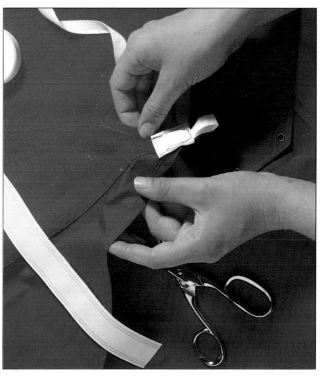

2 Cut a piece of ½in. wide tape to 3½in. long, and trim it to match the shape of the keel at the towing point. Allow ½in. from the edge of the keel for a hem. Sew the fabric tape into position along two sides.

3 Hem along two edges of the keel with a double fold, turning over ½in. in total. Mark two points on the reinforced part of the keel 2in. apart as shown, and punch an eyelet into each (alternatively, attach a tape loop) for the flying line. Take care not to perforate the stitching.

4 Sew a small triangle to a contrasting large one, to form one half of the sail, using a flat-fell seam for strength and neatness. Repeat for the other half of the sail. Place the two halves right sides together, and position the keel between them, 2½in. from the top of the kite. Trim one side of the seam allowances to reduce the bulk of the seam and flat-fell the keel into place. Hem all around the kite using a double fold ½in. wide.

5 For the pockets, cut four pieces of 1¼in. wide grosgrain ribbon or tape to a length of 2½in. and fold each piece as shown. Stitch a pocket onto the bottom of the kite, placing a loop of tape between the kite and pocket to take the tail, using a double row of stitching all around the pocket.

6 *Stitch pockets onto the other three points of the kite, trimming off any fabric that extends beyond the edge of the kite. These three pockets do not need loops.*

7 *Cut two pieces of dowel that will fit the kite snugly, and round off any sharp ends with sandpaper.*

8 *Cut two pieces of narrow tape 20in. long. Stitch the tapes onto the back of the kite at the junction of the two spars and at a point 14in. further down. Tie the tapes over the spar and the spine.*

9 *To make the tail, cut 15 red and 15 blue pieces of fabric 3½in. × 6in. Cut on the bias to lessen the risk of fraying. Pin alternate colors onto the narrow tape at 8in. intervals, ruching each piece to make a bow shape, and stitch securely into place.*

10 *A fishing swivel hook sewn onto the end of the tail will help to prevent it from knotting up in the air. Alternatively, the tail can simply be tied onto the loop at the bottom of the kite.*

Attach the flying line to one of the eyelets in the keel (the top for lighter winds and the bottom for stronger).

80